SUN, STONES AND

SILENCE

By DOROTHY HALES GARY

Introduction by Georges Duhamel of the Académie Française

Text by ROBERT PAYNE

SIMON AND SCHUSTER · 1963

PUBLISHED BY SIMON AND SCHUSTER, INC.
ROCKEFELLER CENTER, 630 FIFTH AVENUE
NEW YORK 20, N.Y.

FIRST PRINTING

LIBRARY OF CONGRESS CATALOG CARD NUMBER: 63-13766
PRODUCED IN COLLABORATION WITH CHANTICLEER PRESS
PRINTED BY AMILCARE PIZZI, S.P.A., MILANO, ITALY

To my son, Robert

Sun, Stones and Silence

Who does not know Egypt in winter and summer,
Who does not know the lands of the Near East,
Who does not strive to understand the origins of Western
    Civilization,
Who has no feeling for the past—
Such a man can never understand the three words in the
    title of this book:
But those who recognize these words and contemplate
    these pictures
Will come to know humanity better, and themselves as
    well.
Honor then to Mme Hales Gary who by her talent has
    enabled us to see the world we live
    in.

Soleil, pierres et silence

Qui n'a pas visité l'Egypte, en hiver comme en été,

Qui ne connaît pas les pays du Proche-Orient,

Qui ne cherche pas à comprendre les origines de la civilisation occidentale,

Bref qui ne s'intéresse pas au passé du monde humain ne peut comprendre les trois mots qui servent de titre étrange et frappant à cet ouvrage.

Mais qui connaît ce texte et qui tourne les feuillets de cet admirable album a bien des chances de bien comprendre l'humanité et de mieux se comprendre lui-même.

Honneur donc à Mme Hales Gary qui nous a, par son talent aidé à nous représenter le monde où nous vivons

Duhamel

SUN

In the Hall of Records built at Karnak there is a granite column on which an unknown sculptor once carved three papyrus flowers. Today the weathered granite shines with a smoky yellow color, rich and luminous under the Egyptian sun, and there is nothing in the least remarkable about this column except its strange simplicity and the legendary life which seems to flow from it. Those three long-stemmed papyrus flowers have a modern look about them, very taut, very clear, the clean stems shooting upward in high relief, not nervous or restless in any way. There are no inscriptions, no decorative elements except the faintly incised shapes of the petals. There are only the three flowers, and those the commonest in all Egypt!

It is worth while to pause a few moments before this column which is almost lost amid the myriad stones of Karnak. There is a monumental elegance in those three stems capped by the flaring flowers, and without knowing anything about them one might guess they were heraldic emblems with an ancient history, and possessed a special significance in the Hall of Records. Thirty-five centuries have passed since this column was erected in the reign of Tuthmosis III, but those flowers, that emblem, were already old in his time. For centuries sculptors had been carving these flowers in very much the same way, though without this soaring power and calm magnificence.

We know the history of this column; we know all its ancestors. Almost at the moment when the Egyptians first carved in stone, in the Third Dynasty, about 2800 B.C., we find slender papyrus columns in the mortuary complex of King Zoser at Saqqara. They are the earliest stone columns known to us, and therefore they stand at the beginning of our architecture. The great clustered columns would

9

follow, Ionic and Corinthian would come to full flower, Gothic columns would soar heavenward until they lost themselves in the roof shadows. But in the beginning there was the column in the shape of the papyrus, long-stemmed, with the cuplike crown.

Most of our beginnings can be traced to Egypt. There, if anywhere, we have our origins, in that narrow land which was scarcely land at all, for it embraced little more than the banks of the Nile. For countless ages these banks have been crowded with generous thickets of dark green papyrus sometimes rising to a height of twenty feet, eternally rustling and creaking, eternally in motion. The waterfowl nested in the shadows of the papyrus forests, which gave shade to men and beasts. Out of those long slender grasses the ancient Egyptians made nearly everything they wanted. The roots were food and sustenance. From the stalks they made boats, mats, ropes, sandals and cloth. Bound together, they made posts; woven, they produced roofs. Cut into fine strips, laid crisscross and pressed together, papyrus became paper. Cradles and coffins were made of it. These tough fibers were the supreme gift of the Nile, beautiful, useful, needing no care, free to anyone who had the strength to pluck them, and because they possessed all these properties, and were ageless and deathless, the people of Lower Egypt came to regard them with the pride reserved for those objects which are so precious that life is unthinkable without them; and the papyrus became their emblem. In much the same way the lotus became the emblem of Upper Egypt.

In the Hall of Records at Karnak the papyrus column does not stand alone. Close to it is the lotus column, carved in the same manner, very quiet and noble, with the petals delicately rounded, pointed, and flared. Yet the papyrus column is incomparably the more beautiful, perhaps because it is simpler. There is only the stem and the cuplike flower, the abstract image of a flower, the sense of some splendid thing leaping heavenward. These two columns supported the roof of one of the chambers where the records of the reign were kept. Together they represented the power and might of all Egypt.

In the days when this Hall of Records was built, Egypt was the greatest power on earth. Her armies were ravaging Asia. Prisoners and tribute-bearers flocked to the court of Pharaoh. Daily reports were compiled, battle lists were prepared, and the scribes and secretaries were continually drawing up catalogues of treasure from the conquered territories. The Hall of Records was the nerve center of an expanding empire. At this time the Egyptians had reached the Euphrates and the Fourth Cataract of the Nile. They had conquered Cyprus and their ships sailed unhindered among the islands of the eastern Mediterranean. In the quiet fervor of his victory hymns Tuthmosis III proclaimed that the entire world belonged to him, or rather to the god Amon-Re who was his protector and in whose honor he built the temple at Karnak. He ordered the image of Amon-Re to be carried into the battle lines. In the name of the god all decisions were taken, and all victories were ascribed to his intercession. Amon-Re was "the hidden one," the mysterious and invisible generative power of the Sun, creator of all things, and he was depicted as a handsome youth crowned with the solar disk and two immensely long feathers. This youthful Zeus with the face of Apollo presided over the Egyptian victories. In the inner sanctuary of the temple he conversed with Pharaoh, who regarded himself as the human aspect of the god.

Like many conquerors Tuthmosis III was a man of strangely feminine temperament. His features were delicate, almost girlish—full lips, a prominent aquiline nose and cowlike eyes. He had the look of a dreamer who dreams dangerously, gentle and violent by turns. According to his own account inscribed on the walls of Karnak, scarcely a year passed but he was waging implacable war against his enemies, and since he reigned for more than half a century the number of his wars was almost beyond counting. Long before he died, the treasuries of the Temple of Amon-Re were crammed with the wealth of Asia, and all the kings of the border lands were sending tribute.

The Pharaoh saw himself as a benevolent and inspired visionary determined to extend the bounds of Egyptian civilization. He invited the princes of western Asia to his court, taught them Egyptian sciences, and encouraged them to worship Amon-Re. There was a constant traffic of embassies between his capital at Thebes and the barbaric tribes of the border lands. It was one of those great revolutionary epochs when nations are compelled to confront one another and learn from one another, and when a kind of cross-fertilization occurs. In the reign of Tuthmosis III Egyptian civilization came to its full maturity.

The evidence of that maturity lies in all the surviving relics of his reign. The sculpture of his age has a fullness, an amplitude, a grandeur, which testify to a serene confidence in the future and a sense of harmony with the world. It is all strength and controlled power, the leaping masculine stems married to the rich feminine curves of the flower. There is no sense of urgency: only of calm accomplishment enduring forever.

Yet these three flowers are not what they seem to be; secrets lurk in them, and they speak to us across the centuries about a way of life which has departed from the world. At first glance they appear to have been carved naturalistically, but we learn better at a second glance, for no papyrus flowers ever possessed these proportions. What we see is the abstraction of a flower produced in a vivid and dynamic age, and though these flowers are the traditional emblems of Lower Egypt, the presence of Amon-Re has subtly altered them. Almost they are prayers, hands reaching up to "the hidden one," and their maturity is not of this earth. They rise in splendor toward a greater splendor, like hymns toward the Sun.

11

For four thousand years the Egyptians worshiped the Sun, which is not to say that they were sun-worshipers. Just as the Nile, the tangible bluish-gray river which rose in flood during the summer months, issued out of a heavenly Nile which perhaps encircled the sky, so the Sun they worshiped was even more splendid, dazzling, and fruitful than the sun which they saw every day. In spite of the innumerable names they gave to the Sun, and the strange animal-headed gods who presided over their hearths and sat enthroned in their temples, they were as monotheistic as the Christians who worship a single Lord while paying continual tribute to the Virgin and a host of saints. All through Egyptian history we are made aware of a single creative force divinely moving and permeating the universe, worshiped in the shadowy temples, celebrated in hymns, beloved by the common people. The heavenly Sun in its rising and its falling was the object of their adoration. They saw themselves as children of the Sun, whose servants they were, and in honor of the holy Sun they celebrated feasts and went on joyful pilgrimages and made offerings of bulls and flowers and incense. For them life was a perpetual ceremonial. Herodotus called them "the most religious of men," and so they were, but their religion was almost wholly concerned with the worship of the Sun in its various manifestations. Every morning was an adoration of the risen Sun, and every evening they worshiped its decline, knowing it would return on the following day; and they especially delighted in the Sun on the horizon with its fierce explosions of colors. In Egypt the dawn comes like a dramatic lifting of curtains, the beating of drums. Suddenly the land from being quiet resounds with energy. In the evening as the sun sinks there is a sense of haunting melancholy. *The Hymn to the Sun,* written by the heretic King Akh-en-Aton, is a perfectly accurate description of the Sun as it rises and falls over Egypt:

> Lovely is Thy rising on the horizon of heaven,
> O living Aton, Thou who givest life.
> Thou risest in the eastern sky,
> And all the land is colored with Thy loveliness,
> For Thou art splendid, mighty, and beautiful,
> Being uplifted over all creation.
> Thy rays embrace the earth and everything made by Thee.
> Thou art Ra, and all are made subject to Thee
> For the sake of Thy beloved son.
> Thou art afar off, but Thy rays lie on the earth.
> Thou art in the faces of men, and they watch for Thee.
>
> When Thou settest on the western horizon of heaven,
> The earth sinks into the darkness of death:
> Men sleep in their chambers with their heads covered,
> And no eye can see another.

If all their possessions were stolen under them,
They would know nothing of it.
Every lion cometh forth from his cave,
And the serpents murder with their fangs,
For the darkness is their habitation.
The earth lies silent:
He who created them sleeps in His horizon.

When the earth brightens, Thou risest on the horizon,
Thou shinest as the Aton of the daylight.
Thou drivest away the darkness.
When Thou sendest Thy rays,
The Two Lands rejoice,
Men awake and stand on their feet,
For Thou hast raised them.
They bathe their limbs, they put on clothing,
They raise their arms to adore Thy rising,
The whole earth goes to its work.
The animals lie asleep on their pastures,
All trees and grasses turn green,
Birds flutter in their nests
And lift their wings to adore Thy energy.
All the cattle leap to their feet,
All flying and fluttering things come alive,
When Thou shinest upon them.
The ships, too, go up and down the Nile,
For every highway opens to Thy rising.
The fish in the river leap toward Thee,
Thy rays fathom the depths of the sea.
Thou createst the child in the womb,
And makest the seed in man,
Giving life to the child within the mother,
And Thou soothest him so that he shall not weep.
Thou art his nurse within the womb,
Giving him breath so that Thy creatures may live.
When the child is born,
Thou openest his mouth for his crying,
And Thou givest him whatever he needs.

When the chick chirps in the egg,
Thou pourest breath within him
So that he may live,
And when Thou hast made him strong
To break through the egg,
He comes chirping with all his strength
And runs with his feet
When he has come through.

Infinite are Thy works!
They are hidden from our eyes!

Thou art the Only God,
And no other possesses Thy power.
Thou hast created the earth to Thy pleasure, Thou alone!
Men, and all cattle and herds,
All that walk upon the earth,
All that fly in the heavens,
And the nations of Syria and Kush and the land of Egypt.

To each Thou hast given a place:
Thou givest to each one what he needs.
According to the length of his days
Thou hast provided his sustenance.
Men speak in many tongues,
And many are their forms and colors,
And Thou hast made the foreigners different from us.

Thou hast created the Nile in the other world,
And at Thy pleasure Thou hast borne it along
To preserve the lives of the people:
Therefore Thou hast made them for Thyself.
Thou art the Supreme Lord, grown weary in the making of them,
Thou art the Lord of all lands,
Thou art the dawning, the Aton of the daylight,
Rising in majesty.

Thou hast given life to all the far-off nations,
Thou hast set a Nile in the heavens to fall on them,
Thou hast made waves on the mountains like a sea,
Moistening the fields amidst their towns.

How excellent are Thy ways, O Lord of Eternity!
The Nile in heaven is for the far-off nations
And for all the wild beasts that walk on their feet,
But the Nile flows through Egypt from another world.
Thy rays give nourishment to every field.
When Thou risest they live and thrive in Thee.

Thou makest the seasons to work for Thee:
Winter brings coolness,
And summer heat is for the taste of Thee.
Thou hast made the far-off heavens for Thy rising place,
To behold from afar what Thou hast made, Thou alone,
Shining in Thy many forms as the living Aton,
Rising in splendor, moving far off, coming close again.

Thou hast made infinite transformations of Thyself
Through cities, villages, fields, rivers.
All eyes behold Thee in them,
For Thou art the Aton of the daylight in heaven!

When Akh-en-Aton was born, about the year 1380 B.C, the memory of Tuthmosis III, who had died less than sixty years before, was still fresh. The great conqueror had elevated Egypt to a position of supreme power among the nations, and his successors were able to consolidate the empire. Trade flourished; the people on the frontiers were quiet; there was no longer any need for armed expeditions into Asia. At this precise moment, when the earth was almost too calm and civilization had reached a stage of extraordinary ripeness, a young visionary inherited the throne. He was fifteen or sixteen when he decided to abolish the power of the priests of Amon-Re, who had grown wealthy on the spoils of conquest. He had no love for conquest, no feeling for institutionalized religion. Delving in the old texts of the first philosopher priests of Heliopolis, he decided to revive an ancient form of Sun worship, which had come into existence long before "the hidden one." He worshiped "the Sun revealed," which he called "the Aton of the daylight," and represented by a solar disk with long rays reaching to the earth and caressing it with divine hands. According to the dogma of the new faith, Aton was the Lord of the world, not of Egypt alone, though Egypt was especially blessed. His *Hymn to the Sun* follows the established hymns, but subtly alters their character. Instead of the Sun of brooding power and majesty, he introduced the Sun of tenderness and gaiety, reigning peacefully over all the nations of the earth.

Akh-en-Aton's reign was short-lived, but in the space of a few years he was able to encourage a revolution of the arts. The stiff, hieratic patterns were abandoned. Sculptors and painters produced works of enchanted naturalism. The king no longer sat enthroned, stern and implacable. He took his wife in his arms and played with his children, or waved to the crowds outside his window. It was as though the windows were suddenly opened, and the fresh air came sweeping through the palaces. In all the works of art produced in his new capital at Tell-el-Amarna, we are made aware of a vivid imagination at work. These sculptors and painters celebrated life as though they were intoxicated with it, as though a new and more life-giving blood had been poured into them.

The priests of Amon-Re protested vigorously against the new heresy, but there was no heresy. What Akh-en-Aton proclaimed had been part of Egyptian belief for centuries. They had worshiped the Sun of power, but they had also worshiped the Sun of tenderness. "The Aton of the daylight" was no stranger to them.

The imperturbable perfection of Egyptian dynastic art has nearly always prevented us from seeing the ancient Egyptians as they were. We see the Pharaohs looming in their majesty, but we forget the laughter on the faces of ordinary people. They were a fine-boned, handsome, gentle people, naturally peaceful, very sensual, enjoying life to the full. Herodotus observed that after the Libyans

15

they were the healthiest in the world, and he was surprised by their habit of stepping aside for their elders and bowing gravely to one another when they passed in the street. They treated their women as equals, delighted in washing themselves, and loved justice; and perhaps it was these qualities which provoked Herodotus, who thought them the wisest of men, to say that "in their manners and customs they exactly reversed the common practices of mankind." They loved life, and had no fear of death. A papyrus discovered in an Egyptian tomb reads:

> Death is before me today
> Like the odor of myrrh,
> Like sitting under the sail on a windy day.
>
> Death is before me today
> Like the springing of a fountain,
> Like the return of a man from the war galley to his house.

They could not imagine that they would never see the Sun after their deaths, and it pleased them to believe that the Sun shone on the dead, appearing once a day for a brief hour. At that hour the dead shout with joy. "Their eyes open again when they see him, and their hearts exult. He hears their prayers, dispels their sorrows and drives away their cares, and he puts breath into their nostrils."

For thousands of years these happy people worshiped the Sun. They lived by the seasons, and every year was like every other year. Almost they had no history. The same Nile rose and fell, the same stars appeared in the heavens, while they continued to live gracefully and peacefully. In all the world there was never any people so enviable.

17

26

30

39

44

STONES

I spent the day choosing and arranging these photographs, spreading them out over the carpet and marveling at their beauty—for Dorothy Hales Gary has shown an extraordinary feeling and understanding of the arts of Egypt—and I was wondering how the photographs would appear in the finished book and whether modern processes of reproduction would recapture the brilliance of the original prints. So the hours passed, and the photographs gradually fell into the proper order, while the strong sun flooded through the windows overlooking Central Park in New York. Far away through the trees I could see the obelisk of Tuthmosis III, which had stood for centuries in the sacred courts of Heliopolis, and all the while Egypt lay at my feet.

I remember being puzzled and a little awed by the fantastic beauty of these photographs. There was a hallucinatory quality about so many of them, and this came, I imagined, from some peculiarly deep affection between the photographer and the objects photographed. The camera eye was not impassive, for in some mysterious fashion it had acquired the gift of love. The true lover does not flaunt himself or strike dramatic poses: he simply gazes quietly at the beloved in a state of rapture. So it is with these photographs which calmly and deliberately and with overwhelming affection register the presence of the beloved objects. There is no heightening of contrasts, no striving for effect. The guardian falcon, the cluster of papyrus flowers, the women washing in the canal at Badrashein, the temples of Karnak in their shadows, all these are seen as though they were lifted out of time altogether and had entered the timeless kingdom of love.

Artists have quarreled with photography since it was first invented, and the quarrel goes on. I remember tramping the streets of Paris on a rainy day and listening to Jacob Epstein while he thundered against the crimes of photography. "I produce a work of sculpture," he said, "and it can be photographed in a million ways, and all the ways are wrong! Photography has no relationship at all to sculpture! There is nothing plastic in a photograph—it is only a limp piece of paper! A photograph cannot walk around a piece of sculpture! All it does is to look up at you and announce with enormous effrontery that it represents something you have created! In fact it represents only a specious play of light and shadows as seen on a certain day, at a certain moment, by a machine which has no awareness of form or harmony or color. I wish to God the camera had never been invented!"

Epstein had grounds for his complaint: too many of his sculptures were photographed incompetently. I think it was the day after that I went to see Constantin Brancusi, who enjoyed taking photographs of his own sculptures. I told him about the conversation with Epstein. He shrugged his shoulders. "I learn from the camera," he said. "It is like having a third eye." Then he showed me a portfolio of his photographs, and there was the same light in his eyes as when he gazed at his own carvings.

I suspect that everything depends upon the photographer: his patience, his understanding of the mechanism of the camera, his affection for the object he is photographing, and his training in the arts. Dorothy Hales Gary is a painter; her photographs are composed like paintings; they have a resonance and texture which derive from the painter's eye, and a very feminine warmth. She wandered through Egypt with a Rolleiflex, determined to capture the shapes of people and sun-warmed monuments with no assistance of filters and Polaroid lenses, very simply and honestly, surrendering herself to the sheer beauty of the landscape, and whenever she set her camera she seems to have felt: "All this will perish, and so I must record it with all my affection and with all the mastery of my craft of which I am capable. I must photograph because my whole life hangs on it." It is the eternal cry of the artist, who is determined to snatch beauty from oblivion.

As it happens, some of the objects she photographed will soon vanish. The great temples of Abu Simbel are destined to be drowned in the waters of the Aswan Dam, thereby proving that not even the most grandiose monuments are permanent. There on a great yellow sandstone bluff looking down on the Nile near the frontiers of the Sudan, Ramses II ordered a vast memorial to his own

50

glory, and not content with a single towering statue he commanded his sculptors to carve four identical statues. Multiplied four times, he sits enthroned, hands resting on his knees, the eyes gazing far into the distance, the lips formed in a faint smile of benediction, so that he has something of the appearance of a benign Buddha blessing the works of men from the heights of his mercy; but this impression of benignity gives way before the cruel majesty of heavy limbs and powerful torsos. It is not only that they are the largest human figures ever carved, being half as high again as the great Buddha at Kamakura, but the sculptors have deliberately made them appear taller, heavier and more powerful than they are by giving a quite extraordinary prominence to the legs which reach forward like vast hammers, as massive as the temple pillars at Karnak. Power surges from these colossal figures; a man is like a fly when he stands in front of them. Between Ramses' legs stand miniature figures of his children, but these miniatures are twice life-size. The cliff carvings at Abu Simbel are testimony to a king's implacable desire for grandeur, not the ordinary grandeur of monarchs but grandeur magnified. If he could, he would have filled the whole of space, the entire universe, with his image.

What is strange and faintly disturbing is the consummate artistry of the design, the successful accomplishment of his purpose. An entire head and torso have crashed to the ground, another has lost its beard, a landslide has destroyed half the frieze of dog-headed baboons which runs across the top, and the falcon-god Horus, emerging from a small house on a level with the king's head, has lost a leg, but even in its ruined state the monument gives an impression of completeness. New, it must have been almost unbearably monotonous, a cliff-high piston machine working at a regular rhythm. Ruined, its symmetry destroyed, the stone crumbling, it has, at however remote a distance, an oddly human air, as though it partook of human mortality. Those pistons, if they moved, would move cumbrously; he can no longer tread down all his enemies; a few would escape. Soon enough he too will be trodden underfoot and hurled into a lake. Five years from now divers descending into the waters of the Aswan Dam will be scared out of their wits by the sight of four sea-kings looming in the ghostly waters.

Ramses II was a slender, light-skinned, dark-haired man with a curving nose and almond-shaped eyes, who seems to have deliberately modeled himself on Tuthmosis III, indisputably the greatest of the pharaohs, and to have suffered the fate of all epigones. Tuthmosis III was an authentic genius who achieved his great position with effortless strength. He moved splendidly, and a little languidly, through an enchanted world, which continually presented him with the evidence of his own magnificence. On occasions he was gentle and magnanimous, and when he boasted of his victories, we have the impression of a man who regarded a succession of victories as the inevitable wages of divinity. When he rode into battle without armor in his golden chariot, and saw the enemy fall back in astonishment, it was no more than he had expected, and when he returned in triumph to Thebes and accepted the acclamations of the people and entered into the sanctuary of Amon-Re and spoke to the god, he was not surprised when the god spoke to him in return and the priests proclaimed him the equal of the Sun. He possessed a breathtaking self-assurance and a superb dignity, but it is his serenity one remembers most pleasantly.

There was no serenity in Ramses II. He moved in splendor, but it was a splendor achieved by continual striving. He inherited the empire when the northern colonies had fallen into the hands of the Hittites and the black tribes of Nubia were growing restless. The ax-wielding Libyans would sometimes appear in the western Delta, and the marauding Bedouins made lightning raids along the river valley. He ordered them to stop, but the raids went on. Gradually he was able to discipline the Nubians, destroy the power of the Nubian princes, and punish the Bedouins. His most famous battle occurred at Kadesh on the Orontes where, according to his own account, he fell into a Hittite ambush and barely succeeded in cutting his way out after making six furious chariot sorties against the enemy, with only his honor guard to help him. In the hour of doom he found himself praying to Amon-Re in Thebes, and the god heard him and struck such fear into the hearts of the Hittites that twenty-five hundred chariots immediately capsized and the riders fell beneath their horses, and more chariots foundered until "the plain of Kadesh was white with corpses." But curiously the Hittite king Muwatallis remained unapproachable, and the Pharaoh took what comfort he could from the sight of Muwatallis standing "averted, shrinking, and afraid" on the far bank of the river. Ramses returned to Egypt to enjoy his triumph, claiming that all foreign nations were now obedient to him, that by his mere presence he had prevented disaster from overtaking his army, and the terror of his name resounded through the world. This single battle has been described endlessly on the walls of Egyptian temples, and always in strident tones. He protests too much. Those hymns to his own glory, those endless recapitulations of a battle which was a near disaster, hint at his outraged pride.

Some years later, in order to secure the frontier, he accepted the gift of a Hittite princess. She was "fair of face like a goddess," he wrote, adding that such a marriage was "unknown, unheard of from mouth to mouth, not mentioned in the writings of the ancestors." So no doubt it was, but Tuthmosis III would have shown considerably less excitement.

The wars continued until he was middle-aged, and when peace finally came to all the frontiers of Egypt, he embarked upon a vast program of self-glorification. Tuthmosis III had built a great temple at Karnak. Ramses II built another and greater one in his own honor. He built a new capital in the Delta, which was inevitably called Ramses. This city was so vast that "the sun rises on its horizon and sets within it." It pleased him to describe the magnificence of the city and the welcome he received when he entered it, the citizens standing at the doors with gifts of flowers, all begging him never to leave. He had the dictator's temper, never happier than when he heard the applause paid for from the public purse.

Many of the memorials he raised for himself have long since perished in the silt of the Delta, but a staggering number remain. Even today his commanding features, the stern and heavy face of a man who never ceased striving after glory, dominate Egypt. He was luckier than most emperors, for the gods gave him time to enjoy himself. He was nearly ninety, in the sixty-seventh year of his reign, when he died, leaving perhaps two hundred descendants and having outlived his twelve oldest sons. Then he was buried in the Valley of the Kings in a gold coffin enveloped in many layers of coffins, wearing a gold mask with obsidian eyes, surrounded by his war chariots and his thrones of ivory and gold, and the most precious of the possessions he had accumulated during a long reign. A hundred and fifty years after his death the cave robbers entered the tomb and plundered the treasure, of which nothing remains. The tomb guardians arrived in time to protect the mummy, or perhaps the robbers had not dared touch it; and the mummy was removed to an unmarked cave, where it was discovered only in 1881. Now he lies in a glass case in the Cairo Museum, the once heavy face made sharp and delicate with age, the skin like black leather and so shrunken that it seems hardly possible that life ever flowed through those veins: he has become a black stone.

In his life he constructed more monuments of stone than any man before or since. Those forests of stone carvings were his natural habitations, the abode of his lonely ghost. At Karnak he could wander through whole courtyards filled with his own images, seeing himself in the reflecting mirrors of his pride, rejoicing in the endless procession of himself. Not for him the white anonymity of the pyramids, where the kings were entombed in shining tents of white stone, so bright that they gave the appearance of melting into the sun. Before they crumbled, the pyramids were blinding, and so were the obelisks capped with gold and electrum, which resembled flaming candles. Ramses II was determined to shine, not in the sun's, but in his own magnificence. The sight of him walking through his own temples and admiring himself must have been a sight to freeze the blood.

But sometimes—and it would seem accidentally—he showed himself in his weakness. The enthroned figures in the large temple at Abu Simbel admit of no dissimulation. They have the thrust of majestic power. In the smaller temple which he built nearby in honor of his queen Nefertari and the goddess Hathor, he appears under another aspect. Once again there are four towering figures of the king, wearing the double crown of Lower and Upper Egypt. He seems to be emerging from the mountain, his powerful hands falling at his side, naked except for a delicately plaited skirt, a figure of superb arrogance. Nefertari appears beside him, her soft body suggesting an exquisite sensuality; and indeed the two statues of her have the appearance of small ivory dolls enlarged to gigantic proportions. There is the inevitable cluster of royal children at their feet. But if we look closely, we observe that the king is curiously stiff, not yet fully awake, his body constrained by the sloping columns which have something of the effect of coffin walls, and it is not at all certain whether he is advancing out of the mountain or withdrawing into it. He had thought perhaps to give the illusion of a king supporting the mountain, and therefore the whole earth, but instead the mountain encloses him. The arrogance remains, but it is the arrogance of the dead.

The small temple at Abu Simbel was constructed carelessly by unskilled craftsmen, perhaps as an afterthought. Something has only too obviously gone wrong, for the king is hemmed in by the living stone, powerless, no longer in command, at the mercy of the stone's shadow sheltering him from the sun. Afraid of the sun, he appears to be withdrawing into his dream of stone.

Soon the waters will be rising up the length of these colossal figures, as over the centuries the sand climbed up and half covered them, preserving them for us. Fishes will lay their eggs in his eyes, and the lake lichen will darken his shadowy features, and in the silence of the lake a head will fall, and no one will know that it has fallen. Ramses will hardly care. There are so many images of him strewn across Egypt that his image will dominate the land for a few more thousand years.

I was still arranging these photographs when the sun set over Central Park. The obelisk of Tuthmosis III had vanished among the trees, but the ancient light

54

of Egypt still glowed on the carpet, so rich and fine a light that it seemed impossible to believe that it had ever been snuffed out. I remembered Brancusi telling me that he had spent only a single day in Egypt, but that was enough to set him dreaming for the rest of his life. I envied the readers who would spend a day with these photographs, coming to them for the first time.

In our time books of photographs of artistic treasures are like the *Books of Hours* of the Middle Ages: we live by them, and they are our guide. We need far more of them, and we need the world's expert engravers to produce them. More than anything else we need photographers who will submit themselves to the arts of the past and patiently explore them, for they are our heritage, the most precious of our possessions. Even now these dreams of stone may teach us how to live.

60

68

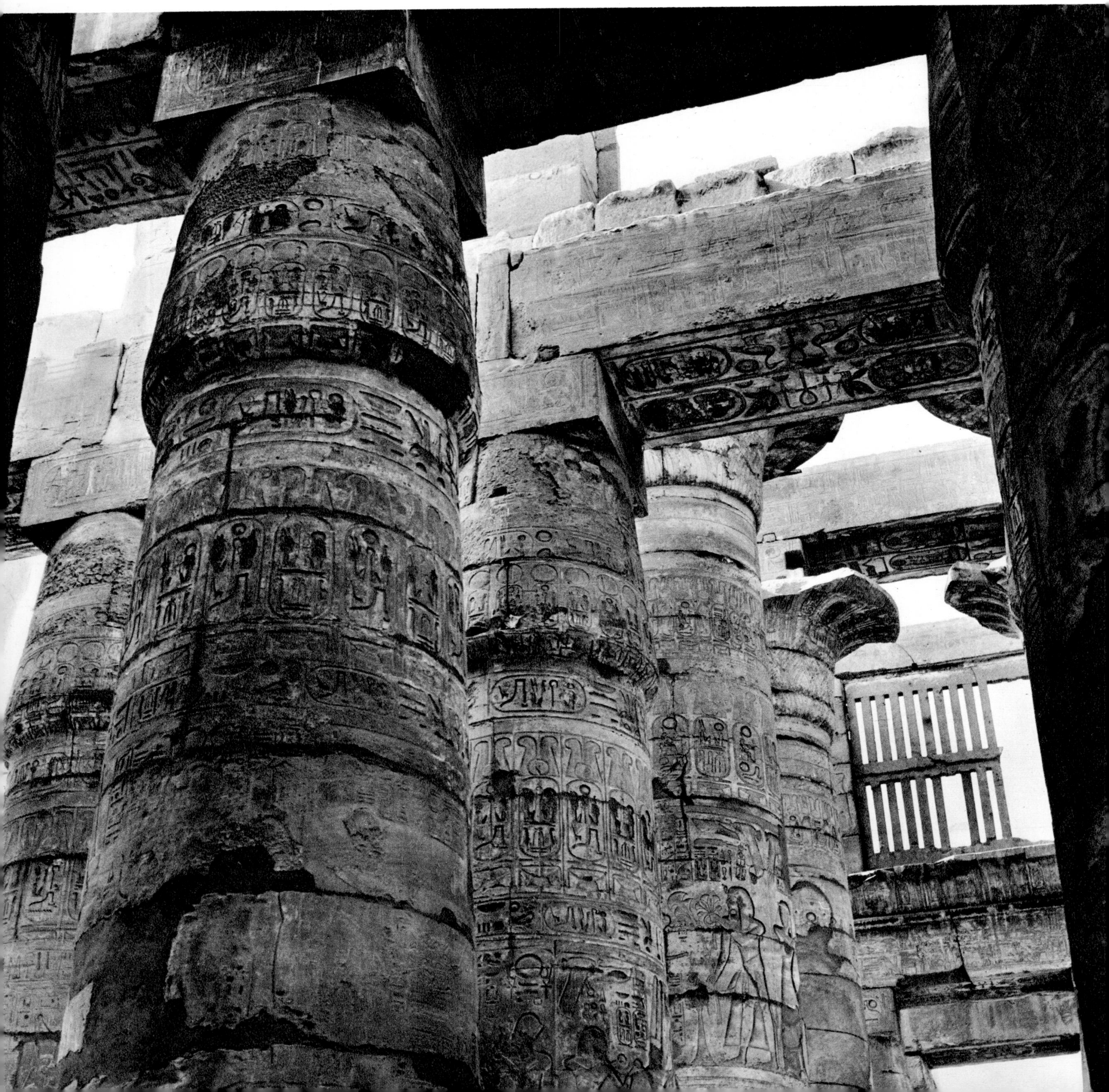

79

SILENCE

Eight years after the death of the Prophet Muhammad a whirlwind emerged out of Arabia. At first it was a very small whirlwind, and the Byzantine Viceroy of Egypt scarcely noticed its appearance. Even if he had been warned, he would not have been afraid, for the whirlwind consisted of perhaps four thousand armed men stealing silently across the desert, armed only with spears and swords, and therefore incapable of taking the great fortified cities of Egypt by storm. The Viceroy might have been more afraid if he had known who was leading the Arabs, and if he could have foreseen that this small whirlwind would gather strength and roar across North Africa and Spain, melting everything in its path.

The leader of the Arabs was a small, thickset man called Amr ibn-al-As, a recent convert to Islam. He was a gifted poet, a shrewd administrator, a general who had already shown his mettle in the wars which led to the Arab conquest of Palestine west of the Jordan. He was a man who laughed easily and well, liking the life of the camp, eating from the same dish as his soldiers, relishing danger, afraid of no one, not even of the Caliph Omar who had given him strict instructions to avoid war with the Byzantine armies in Egypt. The Caliph seems to have known the general would be disobedient and sent a messenger after him with a sealed letter which has become impressively famous in the history of Arab conquests. "If you receive this command before you have entered Egypt, turn back. If however you have already entered Egypt, go forward and seek the aid of Allah." The general, who had guessed the contents of the letter, waited until he had crossed the frontier before reading it. He knew Egypt well from long journeys by caravan in the interior, and he was determined to make an offering of the country to the glory of Allah.

In the humid summer of 640 A.D. the Arabs were encamped outside the gleaming white walls of Heliopolis, the ancient On, most sacred of Egyptian cities, where the Phoenix had its birth and the sacred books were kept. Heliopolis was so old that it was already venerable in the time of Abraham. Though Christianity was the official religion of Egypt under the Byzantine conquerors, the priests of Heliopolis still chanted the hymns to the Sun in the painted temples, and the sound of the chanting floated over the Arab camp. Amr ibn-al-As was in no hurry. He waited for reinforcements to arrive, and sent his spies through Egypt. In the intervals of planning his campaigns he wrote his voluminous and poetic reports to the Caliph, who was unable to comprehend how a whole nation could depend for its life on a single river. "Tell me about Egypt," wrote the Caliph, and Amr ibn-al-As wrote back:

> O Commander of the Faithful, Egypt is no more than
> a desert with two ranges of hills, the one in the west
> resembling sand dunes, the other like the belly of a lean
> horse. Between these hills flows the Nile: blessed are its
> morning and evening journeys. For the Nile has its seasons
> of rising and falling, following the courses of the sun and
> the moon, and causes milk to flow, and gives abundant life
> to cattle. When the springs and fountains are let loose,
> then the swelling waters flood the fields on either side, and
> all the villages are cut off from one another so that the
> villagers must travel in coracles or frail boats or shallops
> light as the evening mist. And when the river has risen to
> the full, it sinks back again, and that is the time when the
> people who have learned to plow the earth so well gather
> the fruit of their labor; and their labor is very light.
> So the crop is grown, and the water is the source of the
> nourishment. Therefore, O Commander of the Faithful, you
> can understand how Egypt is sometimes the color of a white
> pearl, and then like golden amber, and then like a green
> emerald, and then like a carpet of many colors.

So he wrote, that tempestuous black-bearded conqueror, and something of his intense enjoyment comes through the translation, which inevitably loses much of the passion of the original Arabic. It is a hymn to the Nile, differing profoundly from the hymns written by the Egyptians, who never saw the river alone, but always in the arms of the Sun. For the conqueror the Sun was only a small lamp in the heavens, and Allah was greater than all the Suns.

On one day in July 640 A.D. the Arab armies confronted the Byzantine armies led by the Viceroy Cyrus, who was also Patriarch of Alexandria, and soon the Byzantines were in full flight to the north, hoping to find security in the city of Alexandria, in those days the most powerful naval base in the world, and therefore capable of summoning reinforcements from all the cities of the eastern Mediterranean. In Alexandria there were siege works, catapults, heavily fortified battlements. For a thousand years the Greeks and the Romans had been quietly building a city so powerful and so sumptuous that no other city could rival it, gleaming between the sea and a lake, with the beacon fires of the Pharos throwing a red glow over the roofs at night. Here Alexander lay buried, and all the Ptolemies. Here Cleopatra had died, and not long after her St. Mark was martyred, and a vast cathedral was built over the place of his martyrdom. The Arabs camped outside the walls of the white city and waited. The battle of wills had begun. The scholarly and ambitious Cyrus, dogmatic, complicated, accustomed to the intrigues of the court, confronted the simple, poetic Arab from the desert with his rabble army. There were secret meetings, long-drawn negotiations, promises made and then abruptly broken. Cyrus seems to have thought he could retain the position of Viceroy under the Arabs, paying tribute to Mecca instead of Constantinople. He was a weak man, and it seems never to have occurred to him that Alexandria was a prize worth dying for. He signed an armistice with the Arabs, ordered the imperial garrison out of the city, and surrendered. Amr ibn-al-As wrote a characteristic letter to the Caliph. "I have taken," he wrote, "a city of which I can only say that it contains 4,000 palaces, 4,000 baths, 40,000 poll-tax-paying Jews, and 400 theaters." The Caliph was not particularly impressed. When the messenger arrived with the news, the successor of Muhammad listened attentively and then rewarded him with a meal of bread and a few dates.

When Amr ibn-al-As rode on horseback through the Gate of the Sun, passing the mausoleum of Alexander and the palaces of the Cæsars, the history of the world took a sudden turning. The ancient civilization of Egypt which had endured for nearly five thousand years, surviving the Ptolemies and the Roman and Byzantine officers who ruled in the name of distant emperors, came finally to a halt. No more hymns would be sung in the temples of the Sun, there would be no more processions bearing offerings of fruit and flowers and candle-laden boats to the Nile. Islam had come to stay. And when Amr ibn-al-As built a new capital, he deliberately chose a place on the left bank of the Nile, saying he wanted only sand between himself and Mecca.

With the coming of the Arabs the power of Egypt as a civilizing force vanished from the earth as though it had never been. The Arabs themselves were to produce an intricate and impressive civilization of their own, and soon enough they were to learn the benefits of great cities. But except on very rare occasions and at long intervals, Egypt herself produced no works of art, showed no interest or excitement in her past, and remained in a state of torpor. For thirteen hundred years she was to remain on the periphery of power, ruled from Mecca, from Damascus, from Baghdad, from Istanbul, from London, at the mercy of imperial legates and the occasional adventurers who seized power. A long silence fell over her.

In the past the Nile had been the center of the world; now the Nile became a frontier. Once Egypt had been a vast granary, supplying corn to half the Mediterranean, rich with the produce of her soil. But the Arab horsemen had no use for the complex systems of irrigation which had evolved over countless centuries of careful study; and the dikes crumbled, and the canals silted up when the horses trampled the banks. From being the richest country on earth, Egypt became the poorest; and the descendants of Pharaohs eked out a poor living on the ruins of their cities.

The conquerors were not dismayed by the silence which had fallen over Egypt. They had humbled the proud, and took pleasure in poverty. According to an Arab chronicler, one of the envoys of Cyrus returned from a meeting in the Arab camp with a report that he had seen a new and hitherto unimaginable kind of people "for whom death is preferable to life, and humility to prominence, and for whom the world has no attractions at all." He went on to report that they were indistinguishable from one another, the leaders wearing the same clothes as their slaves, and at the time of prayer all knelt on the ground and bowed their faces to the earth in worship of the God they called Allah.

No civilizations could have been more different than those of ancient Egypt and Islam. Egyptian civilization had been predominantly feminine and sensual, in love with the works of time, delicate and complex, dependent upon the seasons and the rise and fall of the Nile. Islam was predominantly masculine, urgent and unyielding as it summoned the worshipers to submit themselves to the timeless will of Allah. There was no rhythm, no pulse-beat, in that world. Allah was the eternal blaze of power, and man no more than a clot of blood which had been given a precarious life by divine mercy. Where the ancient Egyptians saw the world in the embrace of the encircling Sun, a place to be enjoyed, Muhammad saw the world as a purgatory dominated by an unapproachable God, "whose wrath shall enter unto thee." Women, who had enjoyed their near-nakedness, were now enclosed in thick veils. The devout no longer went dancing through the streets. Instead they were commanded to make the pilgrimage across the desert to worship the Black Stone in Mecca, and their sufferings on the journey were accounted as blessings in the eyes of Allah. Though Muhammad himself made no ordinances on the subject, his puritanical followers suppressed the making of paintings and sculptures representing human beings. In the timeless world of Allah only abstract designs were pleasing.

This harsh decree had issued out of the desert: the endless stones and dunes, the endless spaces of the sky. The Arabs were in love with the desert's scentless air, the divinity manifesting itself in the desert silences, the sense of approaching doom which comes inevitably to a man wandering alone across empty spaces. But when the Arabs marched into Syria, Persia and Spain, and confronted the luxury of fertile fields and the panoply of ancient civilizations, they adapted themselves to splendor. Only in Egypt, so close to Arabia, and so dangerous, did they walk like strangers.

In all the other countries conquered by the Arabs and dominated by Islam, the arts flourished, traditions were established, quick and vivid imaginations went to work to soften the harsh outlines of abstractions and sometimes to abandon abstractions altogether. Only the growth of art in Egypt was slow and halting. The fountain had dried up. Sometimes a small trickle flowed, and centuries would pass before another followed. Sometimes, too, the fountain replenished from mysterious sources would unexpectedly deliver a fierce and wonderful flow, as though moved by the sudden memory of forgotten Pharaohs. Most of the Egyptian arts were concentrated in Cairo, where a forest of mosques eventually arose. Of these the greatest were built by foreigners.

The supreme achievement of Islamic art in Egypt was the great Mosque of Al Maydan built by Ahmad ibn Tulun about 876 B.C. Ibn Tulun was the son of a Turkish slave from Ferghana. Sent from Samarra to Egypt to be the lieutenant of the governor, he soon assumed the powers of the governor, and when the people complained that the mosque built by Amr ibn-al-As was too small, he offered to build a new mosque so vast that all the people of Cairo could pray in it. The mosque took the form of a vast square, surrounded by arcades, with a fountain in the center, and a minaret outside joined to the roof by a bridge. The strange *ziggurat*-like minaret was provided with a circular stairway so wide that a man could ride to the top on a donkey, and was evidently copied from a similar minaret at Samarra. An Arab chronicler says that Ibn Tulun was one day toying with a sheet of paper and rolling it around his finger in the form of a spiral when it occurred to him to order his architect to construct the minaret on the same pattern. The story, which was written down by a contemporary of Ibn Tulun, may be true: it is at least possible that the governor of Egypt enjoyed showing his architect how he wanted the minaret built. The minaret is crumbled now, but it must always have had a strange foreign air about it, never quite achieving harmony with the rest of the building.

The glory of the Mosque of Ibn Tulun does not lie in the minaret. It lies in the vast and spacious court and in the delicate arcades with their pointed arches earlier by two centuries than the earliest pointed arches of Christian churches. The mosque suggests a palace, a parade ground, a fortress, foursquare and wholly masculine. In this book there are more photographs of the Mosque of Ibn Tulun than any others, for good reason. Nowhere else in Cairo is there such a sense of controlled and effortless power, of resolute dedication. This mosque stands alone, and all the other mosques of Cairo seem to bow to it.

A little more than a hundred years later the mad Caliph Al Hakim built a mosque now in ruins, though the minaret has survived. His mother was a Christian, the daughter of the Patriarch of Jerusalem, and very early in his Caliphate he seems to have fallen a victim to the war in his blood. This enigmatical blue-eyed Caliph came in the end to believe in his own divinity, and he was murdered in 1021 A.D., no trace of his body ever being found. To this day the Druses of Palestine worship him and look for the time of his second coming. Something of the grandeur of his conceptions can be seen in the minaret with its exaggerated virility as it rises above the walls built by Badr al-Jamali. Strangely, it hints at the great papyrus-cluster columns at Karnak, which he had never seen.

When the slave dynasty known as the Mamluks came to power, ruling with the cruelty of *condottieri*, each sultan dedicated to intrigue because he could not otherwise hope to survive, no one could have guessed that they would encourage the arts. One Mamluk dynasty consisted of Turkish slaves who fought their way to power, the other of fair-haired and blue-eyed slaves imported from the borders of the Caspian. Barquq, the first of his dynasty, was the son of a peasant from the Caucasus, but the tomb mosque he built in his lifetime breathes an air of meditative repose, wholly Muhammadan. Silence broods gently in the courtyard commemorating a murderous sultan. Near the ruined fountain the tamarisks flower, and there is such an air of peace about the place that visitors come for no other purpose than to enjoy the serenity he built out of stone.

Qait Bay was another murderous Mamluk sultan, born in the province of Kipchak on the Volga, kidnaped as a boy, and sold in the slave market of Cairo. He was fifty-five when he came to the throne in 1468 A.D., and one of his first tasks was to build his tomb mosque, completed four years later in red and white stone, the dome decorated with a charming pattern of leaves and rosettes. But though the mosque is pleasing, it is the minaret which has the power to make the heart beat faster. There is a wildness in it and a strength which almost invite disaster, yet this design of archways and fretted balconies, of slender columns and stalactites and intricate arabesques, is brilliantly controlled. It leaps into the air like a fountain of jewels, with a thousand facets to catch the sunlight. There are so many decorative elements in those three separate towers, one springing out of the other, that they are almost beyond counting: one more, and it would shatter into fragments, destroyed by an excess of magnificence. What is this minaret but a sumptuous and slender palace climbing in mid-air? Here the earthly splendor is soaring to meet the heavenly splendor, and like the three papyrus flowers on the column of Tuthmosis III the minaret speaks of a mysterious consummation between the earthly and heavenly powers.

The Mamluk minarets of Cairo are among the wonders of Egyptian art. Where they came from, who invented them, whether they went through a long process of development — all these are unknown. They sprang into existence with the Mamluks, already fully formed, with no known ancestors. There are some who claim they are derived from the Pharos of Alexandria, while others claim they are descended from the Christian bell-towers of Syria, but no one knows the shape of the lost Pharos and the bell-towers have long since vanished. Some Persian and Seljuk influence can be felt, and each of the separate elements has a respectable ancestry. What is breathtaking is the way they are fused together into a single whole of exquisite nobility and grace.

The minaret of Qait Bay is not the earliest of the Mamluk minarets. About 1415 A.D. the former Circassian slave who bore the name of Sultan al-Muayyad Shaykh erected a mosque with two minarets. The mosque has perished, but the minarets survive with their bases embedded in the wall of the Zawilah Gate. The sultan was a notorious drunkard and murderer, who cared nothing for the people he ruled over. Starvation was widespread and beggars filled the streets, while he feasted in his palace. Yet, against all reason, the arts flourished. His two minarets are not the equal of Qait Bay's. They are slender adolescents, striving and thrusting, not quite certain where they are going, a little too eager. Their elegance is virile, but they do not soar effortlessly.

What is Qait Bay's minaret but the papyrus flower three thousand years later? Age has written lines on the face of the flower, but it is recognizably the same, springing from the same soil, obeying the same impulse to embrace the heavens. The world, and men's thoughts on the world, have grown more complex since the unknown artist carved a cluster of flowers in the Hall of Records at Karnak, and these complexities are reflected in the intricate design, but the swift beauty remains. Instead of the three flowers, there are three towers. Instead of three slender stems, there are a hundred stems, and the unfolding flower can be seen again at the very top of the minaret. Out of its flaming nest the Phoenix was born again.

In the silence of the mosque the worshipers kneel and pray, while the voice from the minaret intones the chant of the desert: *La ilaha illa'llah muhammadun rasulu'llah.* "There is no God but God and Muhammad is the Prophet of God." The voice seems to come flowing down from the sky, pouring out of the remote regions of the air, as though sung by angels. In the sudden hush it is easy to forget the savage princes who built these mosques in memory of their own ferocious ambitions. Then it becomes apparent that they were no more than the vehicles through which the artists spoke as they created buildings in honor of God's magnificence. And so at last, in full possession of their inheritance, praying in splendor to a greater splendor, the people came into their own.

109

112

119

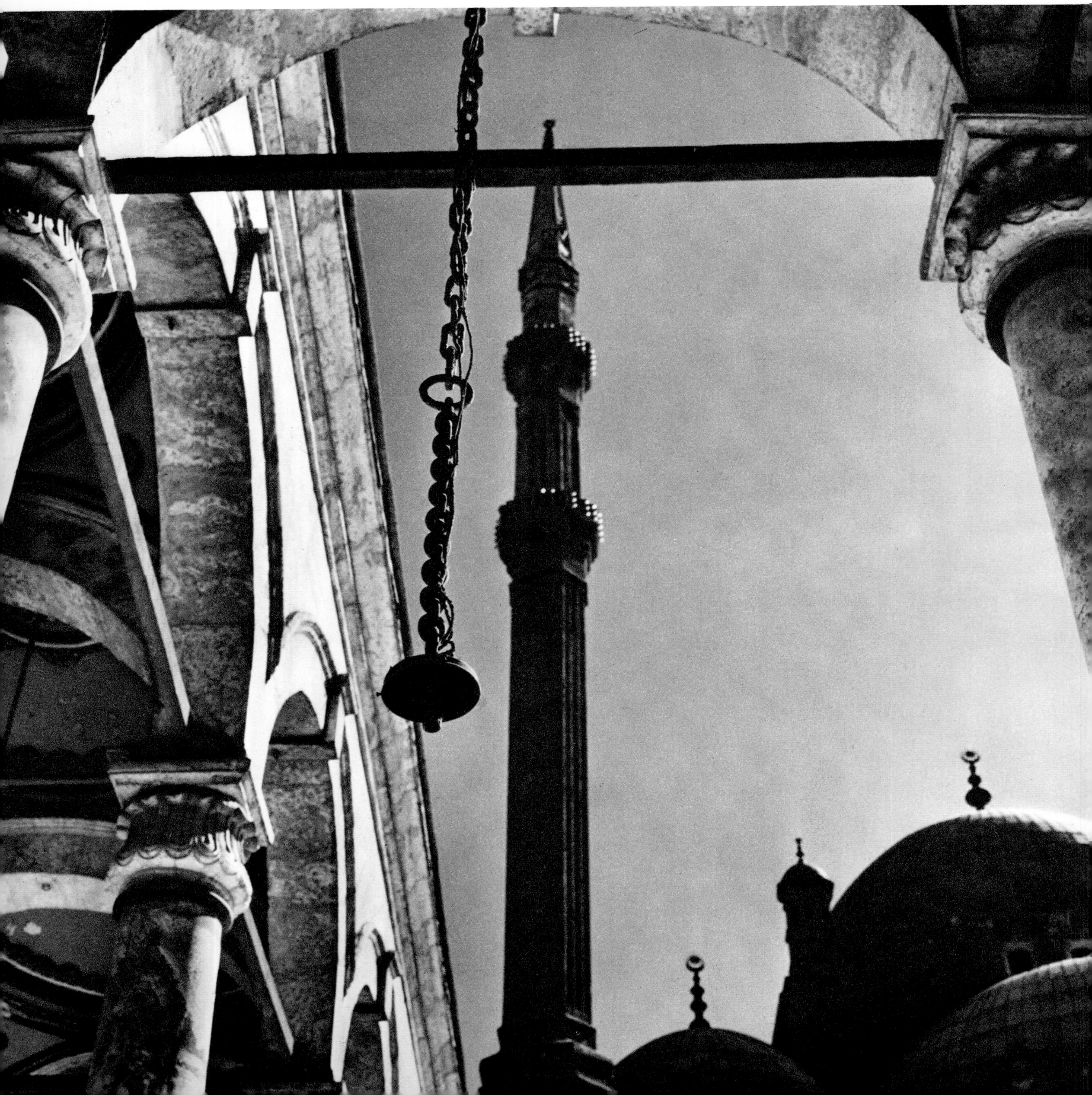

34